# B & M Potterycrafts.

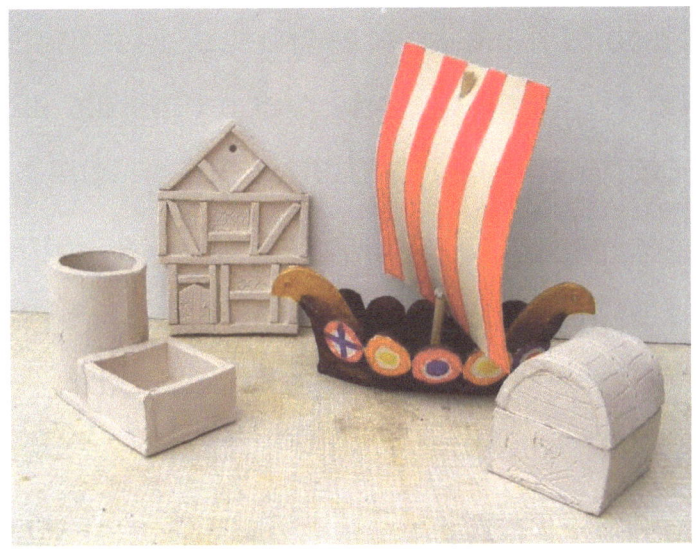

## Slab Pot Modelling.

Create the models shown on this page by following step by step, easy to understand, instructions supported by still photos at each stage.

## Contents.

Roll a slab of clay.

Equipment and tools.

Desk Tidy.

Tudor Houses.

Treasure Chest.

Viking Long Boat.

Brian Rollins.

More projects from:- www.bmpotterycrafts.co.uk

**Introduction.**

Our previous books have concentrated on hand formed models ranging from simple one piece animals such as a hedgehog to elephants using thumb pot techniques.

In this book we are introducing the use of rolling pins to create large flat areas of clay. From the flat clay we cut pieces and shapes and stick these together forming three dimensional structures and figures.

This area of pottery building is classed as slabbing or slab pot building. It enables us to extend our range of models into containers and houses.

This first book of projects introducing basic slab pot techniques is limited to models which have flat edges so that our tool kit contains a plastic knife which is ideal for cutting simple shapes, generally with straight edges.

Follow up books will contain more complex shapes with animal or human forms that are not so easy to cut with a knife.

Each project was written as a stand-alone project and they are available in this single project format from other sources.

This small compendium contains a little duplication of information, generally concerning templates tools and techniques, for which I offer no apologies.

I believe that repeated exposure leads to learning of information and also ensures that students follow all the steps each time which reinforces the basic skills presented in each project.

The Tudor house information gives two extra opportunities to expand on both pottery information and on the variations available in Tudor house building.

Regarding the larger version the student can incorporate their own ideas on design or use the internet to investigate the range of patterns.

The first six pages contain an introduction to rolling slabs of clay, how to prepare templates for clay work and a description of the equipment and tools needed for creating most slab pot models.

Enjoy your clay modelling.

**Brian.**

**Rolling the clay flat. (Create a slab of clay.)**

An important first step is to prepare the clay ready for flattening into a slab, the same steps are used whether you are making a small model or a large model, it is important that you still go through the same process.

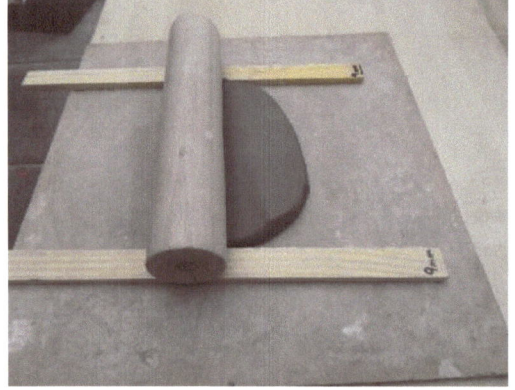

Before using the rolling pin the clay should be made into a round smooth ball.

Take the clay in the palms and remove the largest bumps and lumps by pressing the clay in your hands, similar to making a snowball.

Further prepare the clay by rolling it into a smooth ball between the palms of your hands. Smooth out any cracks in the clay by stroking the clay with finger pressure then re-roll the piece back into a ball shape.

It is necessary to give the clay a smooth surface, free from cracks, because when the clay is further pressed and flattened any cracks will open and appear as a weakness in that area.

If you are working on a table with a plastic laminated surface you can put a final smooth finish on the ball by rolling it gently with the palm of your hand on the plastic surface, I stress plastic surface because using a porous

4

wooden surface will remove moisture from the clay and could make it too hard to use.

Before you flatten the clay with the rolling pin the ball

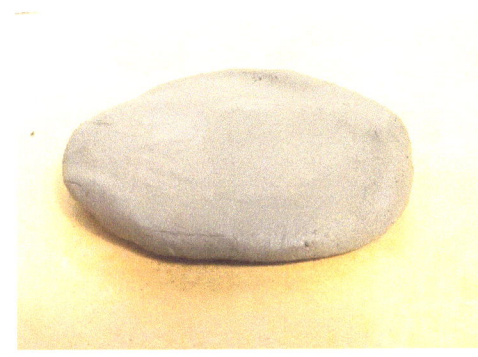

should be flattened by crushing or slapping the piece between your palms making a pancake shape. This pancake shape is necessary because you will find it difficult to start the rolling pin

process with a ball shape.

At this stage check again for any cracks appearing round the edges of the flattened ball due to stressing the clay by flattening it, if any appear repair them with pressure from your fingers. Repeat these checks and repairs throughout the process.

As you can see in the picture the hands are placed on top of

the rolling pin not on the handles, this way you can exert more downward pressure through the clay to the work surface. Use of sticks of a set thickness allows you to produce slabs of clay to a known and uniform

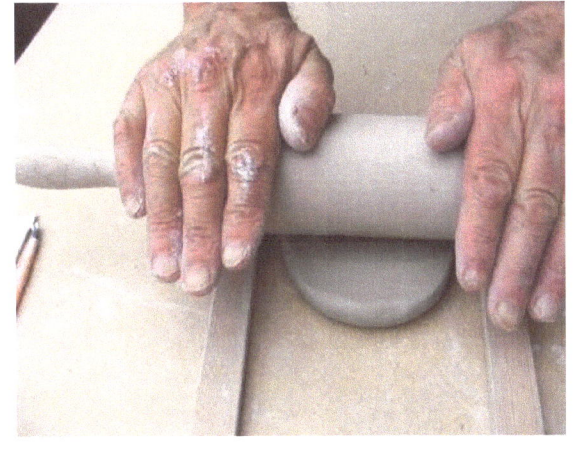

thickness every time simply by ensuring that the rolling only stops when the rolling pin is touching the top of both sticks.

Several times during the rolling it is advisable to peel and lift the clay from the work surface because it sticks to the surface and constant rolling won't make it thinner, lifting and replacing the clay on the work surface allows you to start again and makes the stretching of the clay easier.

Roll out a slab of clay to the required thickness and when the rolling is completed transfer the work to the smaller work surface, ready for cutting.

**Preparation of templates.**

It is good practice to keep the worksheet in clean condition for ongoing usage, the worksheets containing the templates should be copied and used as secondary masters from which you can prepare the templates.

The templates are made from stiff card with one side protected from the clay by a layer of plastic. Cereal boxes ore ok.

Place the worksheet with the templates in position on the card choosing one shape and putting it in a corner of the card to conserve the card space to maximise the number of template

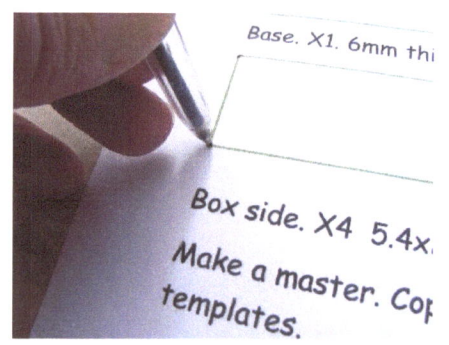

Base. X1. 6mm thi

Box side. X4 5.4x.
Make a master. Cop
templates.

you can make from the card and not to waste the material.

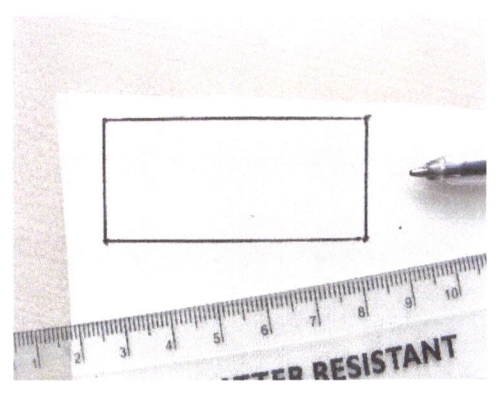

Use a ball point pen to firmly trace the outline of the template onto the card, firm pressure through the paper of the copied worksheet will ensure an outline of the template appears on the surface of the card. If the outline is not clear enough to cut out with scissors enhance it by carefully following the outline with a ballpoint pen.

In the instance shown we are making a rectangle which is relatively easy shape to reproduce as a template.

As you can see in the picture I pressed the pen through the paper and made four hollows on the card at the four corners of the rectangle, I then used a ruler and ballpoint pen to draw the rectangle.

This method was used to create the large rectangle and the straight parts of the base. The rounded end of the base was traced through the paper onto the card and the outline enhanced with the pen to make a clear line for cutting.

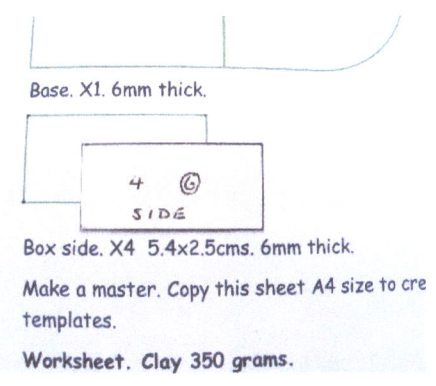

Base. X1. 6mm thick.

SIDE

Box side. X4  5.4x2.5cms. 6mm thick.

Make a master. Copy this sheet A4 size to cre templates.

Worksheet. Clay 350 grams.

The templates are identified by name, quantity and thickness. In the example shown was a Side.

We need 4 of them and the thickness was 6 in a circle denoting 6 mm thickness.

Cut out carefully with good scissors.

Retain the copy of the worksheet as a master and keep the templates for future use as a school resource.

## Work Surfaces and tools.

You will need two work surfaces, one to prepare the clay and one on which to cut the shapes and assemble the model.

The first one is made from 9mm MDF and is at least 15" x 15" (37.5cm x 37.5cm) and the second one is made from 3mm MDF and is 12" x 8" (30cm x 20cm).

I have used these dimensions for years and they are useful for an individual, and in a classroom situation the large one is for sharing one per four children and the smaller one is one for each child which is a personal work surface.

## Tools.

Wooden rolling pin.

2 slats 6mm thick.x20mm wide x 40cms long.

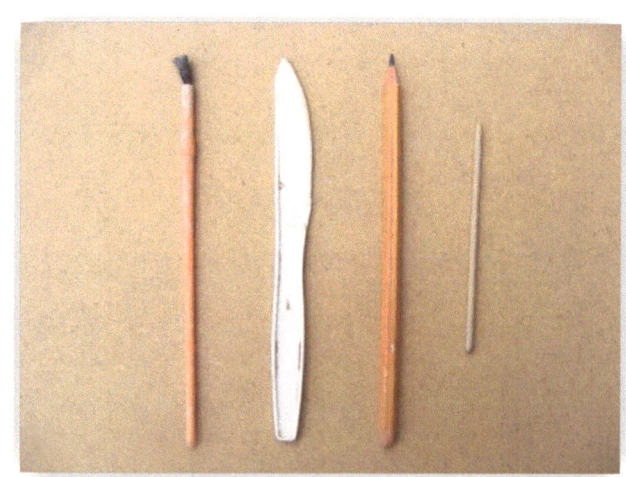

2 slats 3mm thick.x20mm wide x 40cms long.

Stiff paint brush for slip.

Plastic knife.

Sharp pencil or pointed stick.

Plastic knives with the serrated edges trimmed using scissors and sharpened on sand paper are a cheap alternative to a potter's fettling knife and more suitable for use by young children. They are used primarily for cutting lengths of clay but can be used as a spatula to smooth joints between pieces of clay.

Pencils or pointed sticks, shown in the picture, are used for adding details such as eyes or hair to models or drawing patterns and designs on pots of all descriptions. The pointed stick shown was made from 3mm thick skewers used in cooking Kebabs. Cut the skewer to the length you need, I got three from one skewer, sharpen one end and round off the other end using sand paper.

These tools represent a one off purchase as a central resource for a school to be used by any class as required.

# B & M Potterycrafts.

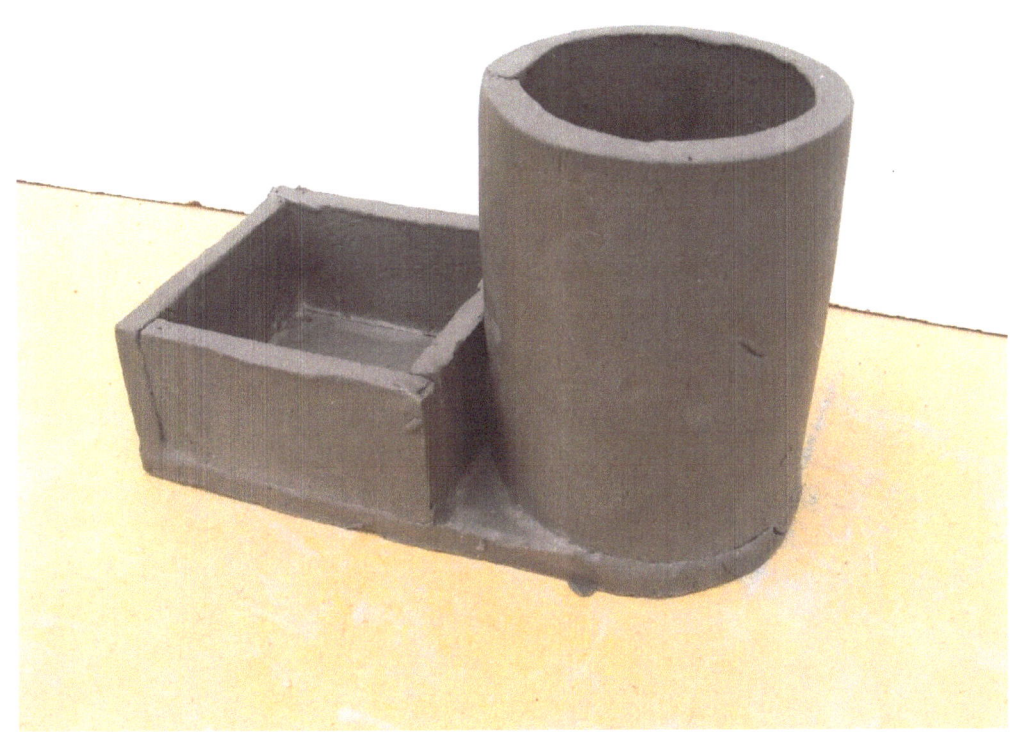

## Slab pot modelling projects.

## Desk Tidy.

Create the model shown on this cover by following step by step, easy to understand instructions supported by still photos at each stage.

### Brian Rollins.

More projects from:- www.bmpotterycrafts.co.uk

# B&M Potterycrafts.

# Building models in Clay.

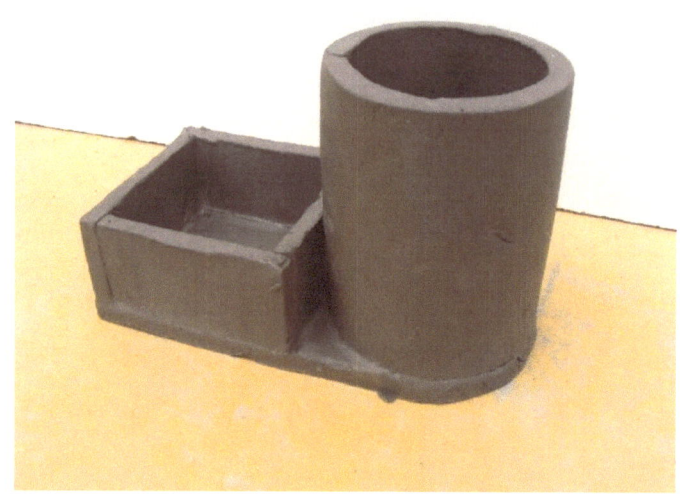

## Desk tidy.

Sequence.

Rolling the clay flat.

Preparation of templates.

Cut out the pieces.

Assemble the pencil pot.

Add cylinder to base.

Assemble the box on the base.

Decorate and design.

Worksheets.

**Roll out the clay and prepare the templates.**

**Page 4 to page 8.**

**Cut out the pieces.**

We are making a desk tidy which consists of a rectangular base with a semi-circular end holding a cylindrical pencil pot and a square box for paper clips and drawing pins.

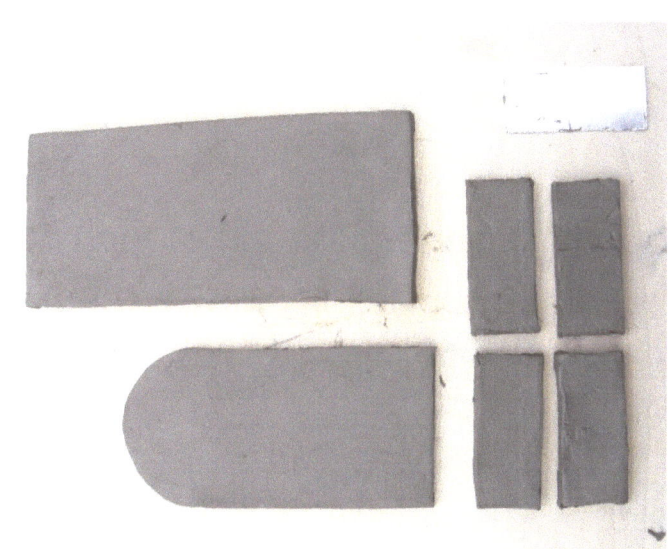

As you can see from the picture the model is made up from six separate shapes.

The large rectangular shape is formed into a cylinder to make the pencil pot and the smaller rectangles make the four sides of a shallow box.

These containers are attached to the base and also attached to each other to strengthen the model.

Place the templates on the clay and cut out the large rectangle, the base and four smaller rectangles.

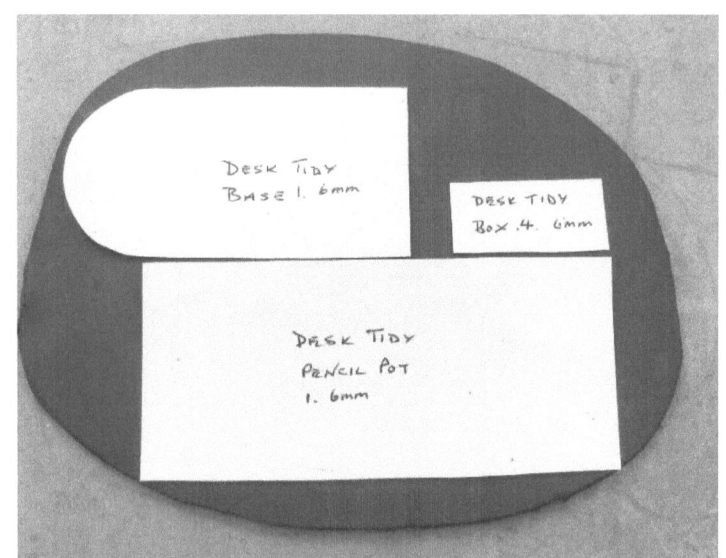

I always use the strategy of cutting large parts first, selecting pieces in reducing sizes. The reasoning behind this is that if you cut out the larger pieces first the slabs of clay remaining will be big enough to cut out all or some of the smaller pieces. However this is less likely to be true if you leave the large piece to the last.

 Templates should always be used with the plastic surface on the clay surface to stop the card soaking water from the clay and softening the card.

As the surface is shiny it also helps to keep the template in place by sticking where it touches while you are cutting around it.

To ensure that the template doesn't move during the cutting process hold it in place with one hand while cutting with the other hand.

It is not vital that all the pieces are cut from that sheet in one go, if you cannot make a pieces or pieces from the bits of clay left simply roll the bits into a smooth ball, pat it flat and roll it out again to cut out the last pieces.

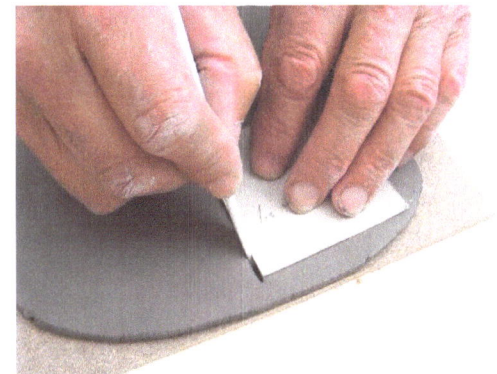

Hold the knife as if you were using a pencil that is with your fingers as close to the point as possible. This gives you more control of the knife point and stops the flexible plastic knife bending away from the clay.

Simply press the knife point through the clay and slide the blade along the work surface to ensure a clean cut, keeping the edge of the knife in contact with the template.

When making slab pot models it is important to keep the cutting edge vertical to the surface to be cut because if the knife is at an angle you will cut under one edge of the slab and over the other edge making them thin in places and difficult to join cleanly to the next piece.

Try to cut in one clean motion, if you stop and restart you will probably leave a jagged edge.


**Assemble the pencil pot.**

As I said earlier the pencil pot is formed from the rectangle of clay formed into a cylindrical shape.

Take the large rectangle and place one of the long sides on the work surface holding the clay upright.

Gently fold the clay into an arc with the long edge forming the arc. Do not force the clay but encourage it to bend by gentle finger pressure until the two short edges are almost touching. Try not to fold the clay or cracks will appear on the fold.

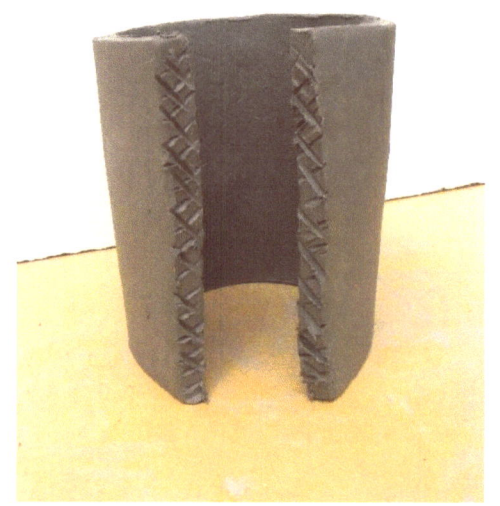

The slightly open cylinder will stand upright at this point.

Place the open edge in a position where you can work on sealing the joint.

This is an important structural joint in the model and to make a solid joint we need to crosshatch the two edges.

Crosshatching is carried out using the tip of your knife with the sharp edge scoring the clay as shown in the picture. Score along each edge in turn, first in one direction and then across the fist marks making a series of crosses.

Crosshatching allows water to penetrate deeper into the clay helping to soften the edges and ensure that when we apply pressure to the joint the clay on both edges fuse together effectively reforming as one piece of clay.

The clay is held together by a material called **slip** which is a mixture of clay and water and it helps the surfaces to bond together.

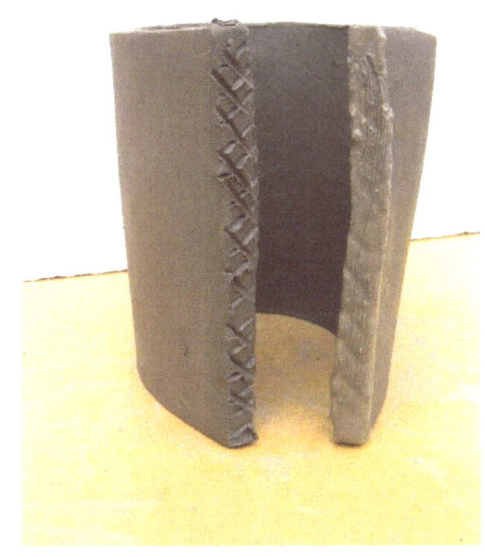

The next picture demonstrates both the crosshatch marks along one edge of the cylinder while the other edge shows how it looks with slip created along that edge.

Both edges should be covered in slip before pressing them together, always apply slip to both surfaces to be joined together.

Dip your brush in the water and rub the brush firmly along the two open edges of the container. This rubbing action and the water creates slip along the surface by roughing up and dissolving the surfaces.

Hold the two edges, one in each hand, in such a fashion as will allow you to press the edges together firmly. You can work from both ends in turn until you have formed a bond along the joint.

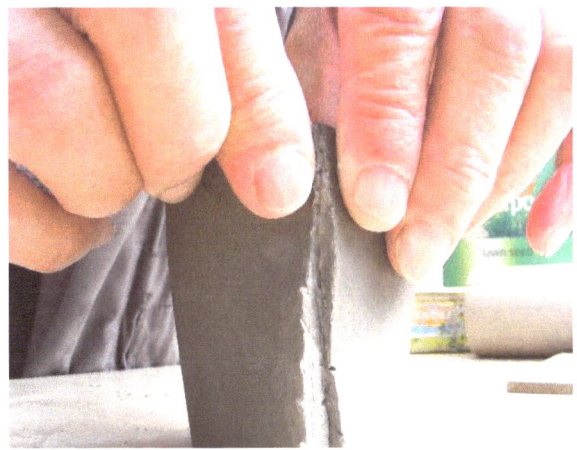

*The creation of **slip** is an important part of joining together two pieces of clay. The water from the brush is rubbed firmly into the clay surface until it turns a lighter grey colour this is the slip and acts as our glue.*

***Crosshatching** is one of the keys to joining two pieces of clay. It consists of the scoring the pieces in the areas to be joined. Use the point of the knife to score the clay.*

*The use of **pressure** is essential in successfully joining two pieces of clay when used in conjunction with crosshatching and slip.*

Smooth the joint inside and out with finger pressure along the seam. Finish off the joint by smoothing the surface with the flat edge of your knife used like a spatula.

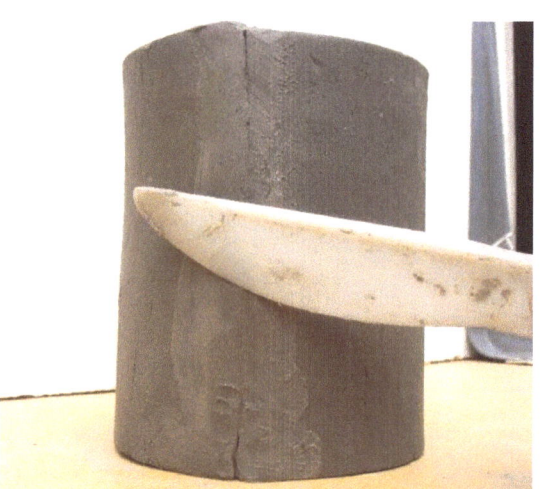

Sealing and smoothing the joint makes it look neat but also serves to strengthen the joint.

**Add pot to the base.**

The fixture can be seen as **structural** and the strength of the whole model depends on the joint, se we need to crosshatch the joint in this case.

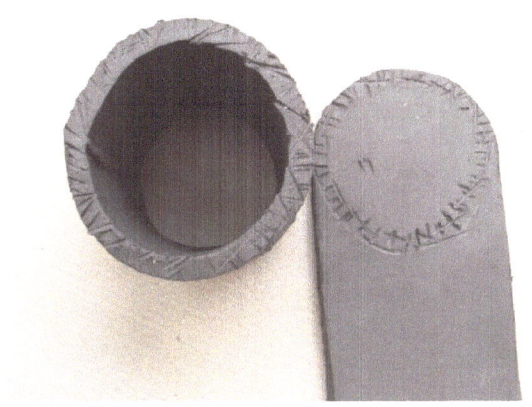

First place the cylinder in position on the base and carefully mark a faint line on the base to identify the area that needs to be crosshatched.

Remove the cylinder and make crosshatch marks inside the circle as shown and around one edge of the cylinder.

Dip your brush in the water container and rub it firmly across the marks adding water to the brush until you have covered all the crosshatch marks and made enough slip to bond the cylinder to the base.

Place the cylinder onto the base and carefully press the cylinder down into the slip on the base.

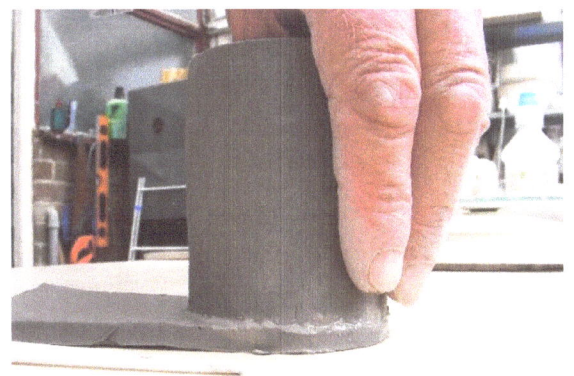

Hold the cylinder as shown and press it down all around to make a good bond.

Strengthen the joint with pressure around the cylinder base.

## Assemble the box.

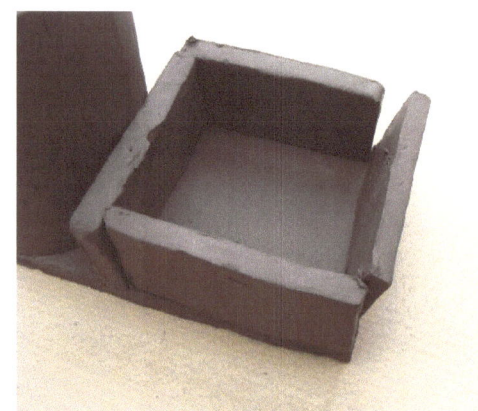

The four rectangles are shorter than the assembled box because this method of assembly means we can use a template of one length to form the square box, the extra length is gained by the thickness of each piece adding to the template length.

To check the assembly method before applying slip place the four sides as shown in the picture.

You can see that each side is aligned to one edge of the base and each piece is bonded to two other sides and to the base forming the box.

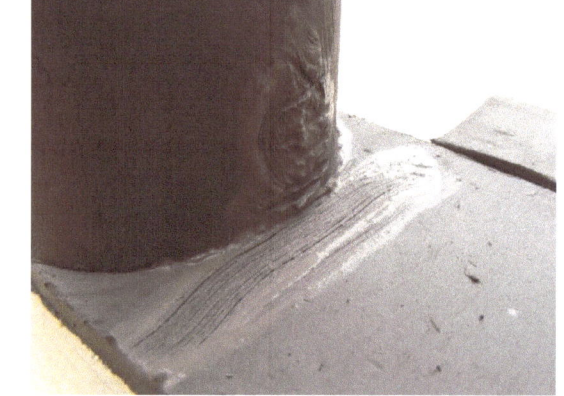

To strengthen the whole assembly we bond the box to the cylinder, in fact we start the assembly process by crosshatching the cylinder and a patch on the first piece of the box.

Apply slip as shown to the cylinder, the base and along one side of the first piece and as we said a crosshatched and slipped area on the back of the first piece.

Slide the side into the slip on the base and align it with the edge of the base finally press the slip on the side piece into the slip on the cylinder. This first piece is now firmly attached to the cylinder and can be used to hold the next piece.

Make slip along the base and the side piece and this time along the edge and side of the two pieces where they join.

Don't forget we always apply slip to both pieces to be joined together.

Repeat this with the third and fourth sides remembering to stick the edge of the fourth piece to the side of the first piece to complete the square.

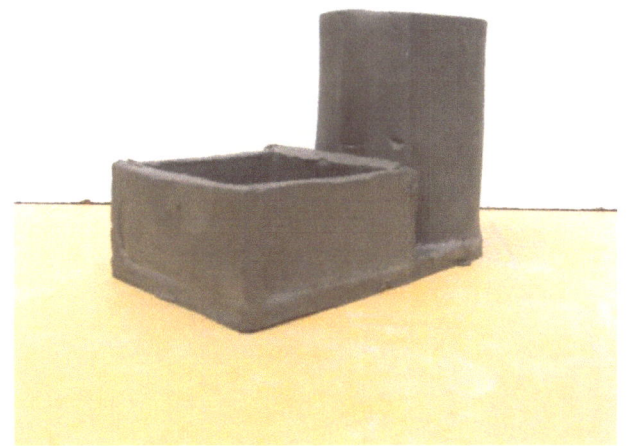

### Decorate the model.

Decoration of the model is dependent on its intended use and who is going to be using it.

Is it to be used on your desk at home, school or in an office,

is it for a boy or is it for a girl?.

You can use the pointed wooden stick or a pencil to impress patterns in the surface of the clay or make flowers or shapes to stick onto the surfaces or wait until it is fired or dries hard and paint your decorations on the model.

Desk Tidy. Templates.

**Clay 300 grams.**

Note. Print this pdf page 'Actual Size'.

DESK TIDY
PENCIL POT
1. 6mm.

DESK TIDY
BASE 1. 6mm

DESK TIDY
BOX .4. 6mm

# B & M Potterycrafts.

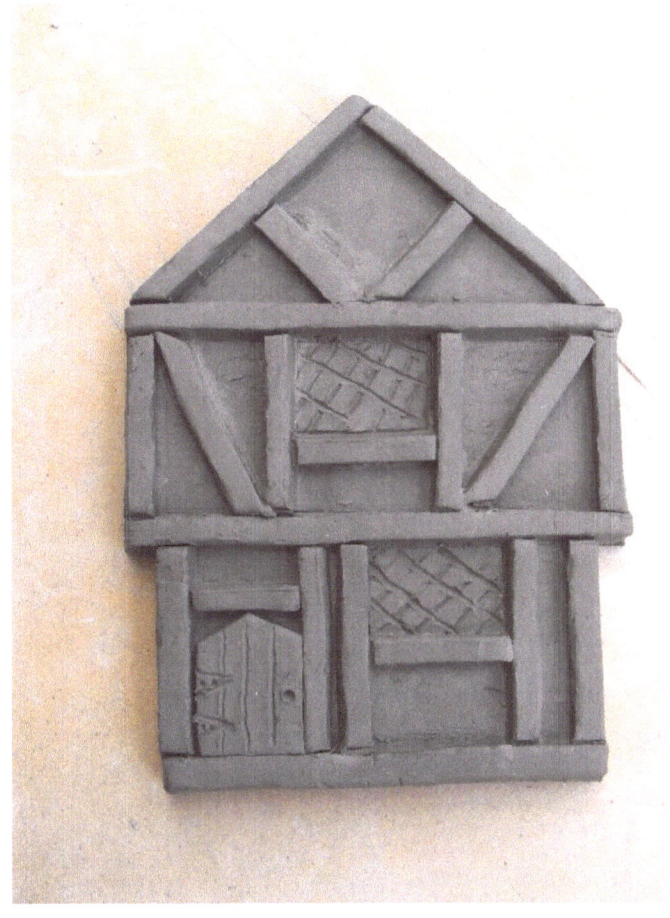

## Slab pot modelling projects.

## Tudor House.

Create the model shown on this cover by following step by step, easy to understand instructions supported by still photos at each stage.

Brian Rollins.

# B&M Potterycrafts.

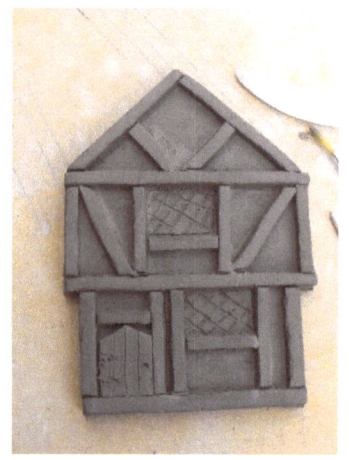

# Slab pot modelling projects.

# Tudor House.

Sequence.

Rolling the clay flat.

Preparation of templates.

Cut out the house shape.

Cut and fit first three strips.

Cut and fit the outer frame.

Door and windows.

Cut and fit uprights and cross pieces.

Decorate and design.

Worksheets.

Materials, Work Surfaces and Tools.

**Roll out the clay and prepare the templates.**

**Page 4 to page 8.**

**Cut out the house shape.**

The templates are identified by name, quantity and thickness. In the example shown we only need one house shape and it should be 6mm thick.

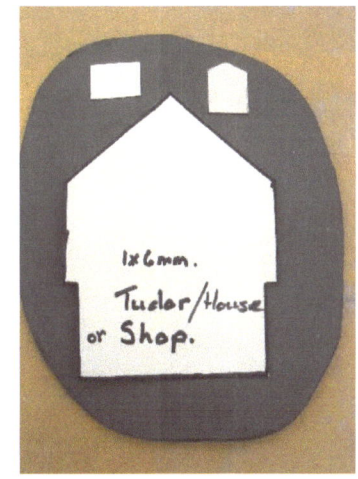

Cut out carefully with good scissors.

Retain the copy of the worksheet as a master and keep the templates for future use as a school resource.

First place the newly rolled slab of clay on a dry area of your work surface.

Always remove the clay from the surface on which it is rolled because newly rolled clay sticks to the board and if the shape is cut before it is moved to a dry surface the shape will stick to the board and will probably be damaged in removing it.

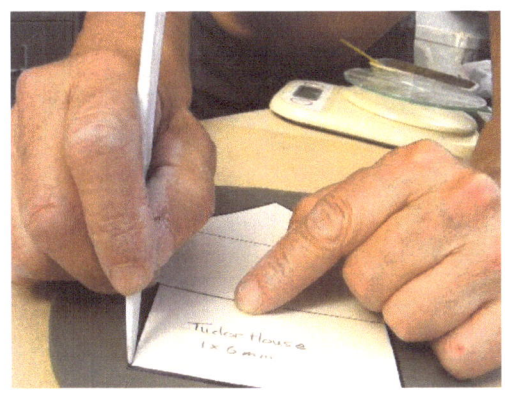

Hold the knife close to the point as shown in the picture and use the tip of the sharp edge to cut the clay.

Press the knife point through the clay and draw the blade

along the edges of the shape keeping the side of the knife touching the card while you are cutting the clay.

Hold the template still with one hand while you use the knife with the other hand.

Start each cut away from your body and draw the blade through the clay towards your body. I have found this method easier and more effective than pushing the point away from my body.

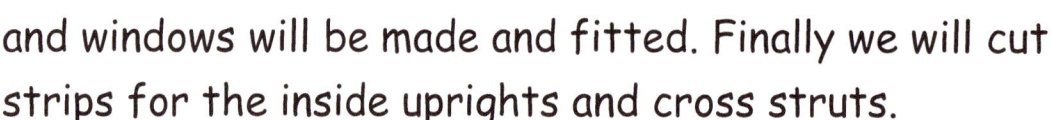

We will add the structures which define the building in several stages.

First we will add the three main cross beams. Then outline the uprights and roof joists, the door and windows will be made and fitted. Finally we will cut strips for the inside uprights and cross struts.

To complete each stage we will use slip to fix the pieces in place.

**Cut the first three strips.**

The first three strips will form the horizontal crossbeams, one to build the flooring on, one to help support the first floor and the third which will help to support the roof.

The first step is to prepare the clay for rolling flat using the techniques described for making the house shape.

Roll the clay into a smooth ball, pat it fat and finally use the rolling pin and sticks to make a 3mm slab from which we can

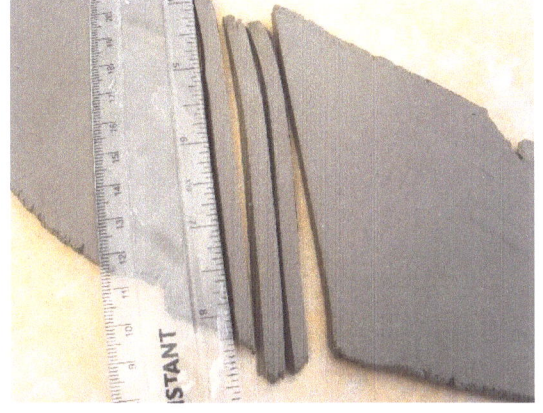

cut the pieces.

The slab of clay needs to be wide enough to produce these first three strips as they will be the longest ones needed, all the others will be long strips cut to the various lengths needed to build the structure.

As you can see from the picture the three strips have been cut at a slight angle to make the strips long enough to fit across the house.

Lay the three strips in position, one above the floor level, the next along the line that defines the first floor and the third strip lined up with the start of the angle of the roof.

Use you plastic knife to trim the strips to the correct length and stick each one in position with slip.

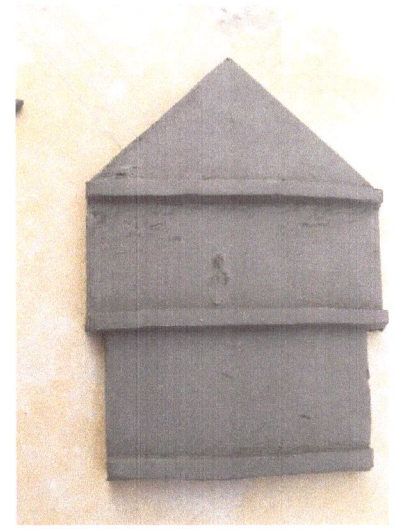

Remove each strip in turn, dip your brush in the water and rub the brush and water along the area where the strip will be refitted. Repeat this on one side of the strip. These wet areas will be made shiny with the water and the shiny material is called **slip** which helps the clay bond together. To complete the joining press the strip in position with your finger or thumb.

The slip and the pressure make the clay pieces bond together.

**Make and fit the outer frame.**

The outer frame is made up from shorter pieces than the horizontal crossbeams but you can follow the cutting sequence and continue to produce longer pieces which can be trimmed to fit the outer frame. Prepare and cut all the pieces before finally sticking them in place. As you can see from the picture where the piece fits at an angle to the next piece the clay is also cut at an angle to give tidy joints without too much space in between.

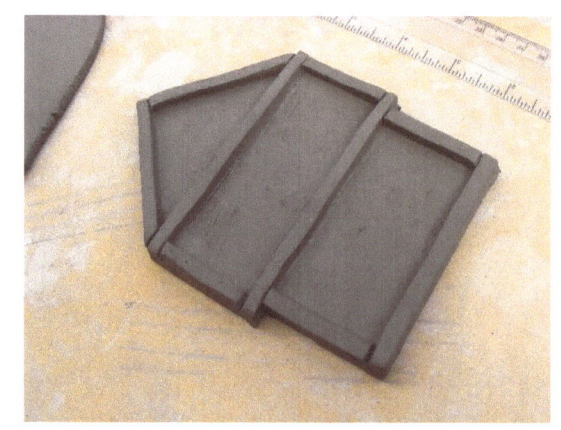

Prepare the strips as shown then remove them one at a time, add slip to the house and to the strip, position the strip then press it firmly into place.

Continue in sequence round the frame until all the pieces are fitted.

You now have a framework which helps you to position the rest of the structure.

## Doors and windows.

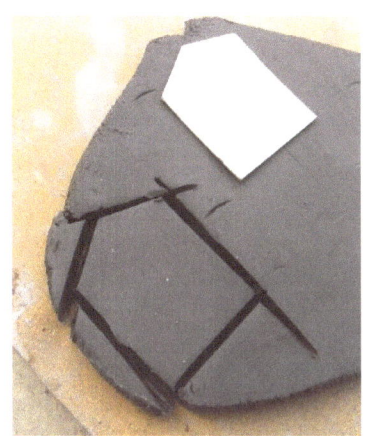

Cut the door shape from the 3mm piece of clay, remembering that you still need more strips to complete the structure so cut the door from an area of clay that is not suitable for strips.

Create a suitable patch of slip in the bottom left hand corner of building and also on the back of the door shape. Position the door and press the shape firmly into the corner.

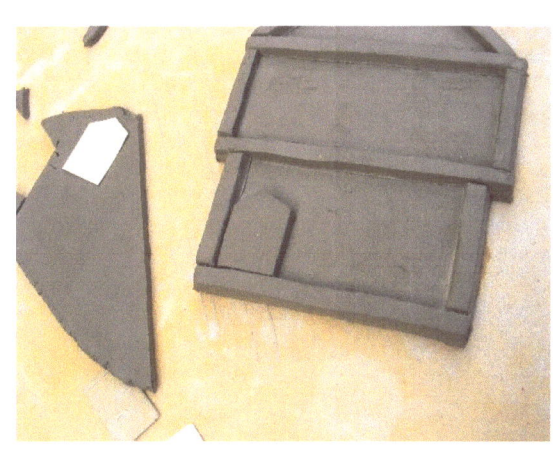

Window shapes are not cut out but are traced onto the surface of the clay and window frames are made to fit around the windows.

In this demonstration we are making one window on the ground floor and one on the first floor.

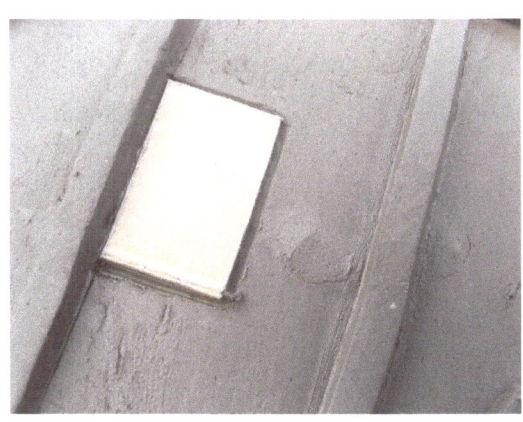

Place the window template in position and use a sharp pencil or pointed stick to make an outline of three sides of the shape as shown.

In Tudor times window glass was expensive to buy and could only be made in small pieces and were either square, rectangular or diamond shape held together with strips of lead.

We are representing these windows by drawing diamond patterns across the window area with a sharp pencil or a pointed wooden stick.

Make the lines carefully and do not press too hard which will make the lines too deep in the clay and weaken that area.

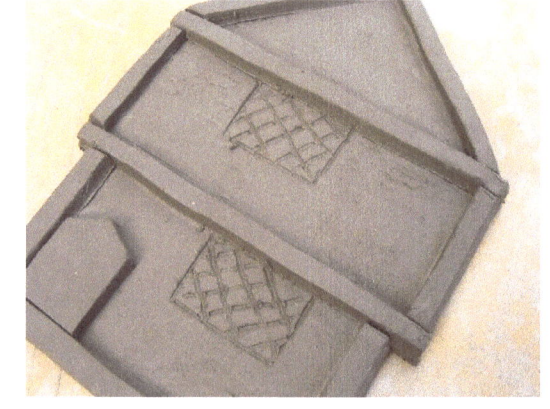

As I said the windows can be made as small rectangles or squares by gently drawing lines across the window area.

It is your model so you are free to decide on the pattern that you prefer.

**Cut and fit uprights and cross pieces.**

Cut several more strips in preparation for fitting the final pieces as window supports, uprights or diagonal supports.

Use the strips to make the door frame and uprights for the windows. Cut the pieces to the correct lengths and place them in position before making slip to fix them in position.

When frames are firmly fitted into place make and fit the

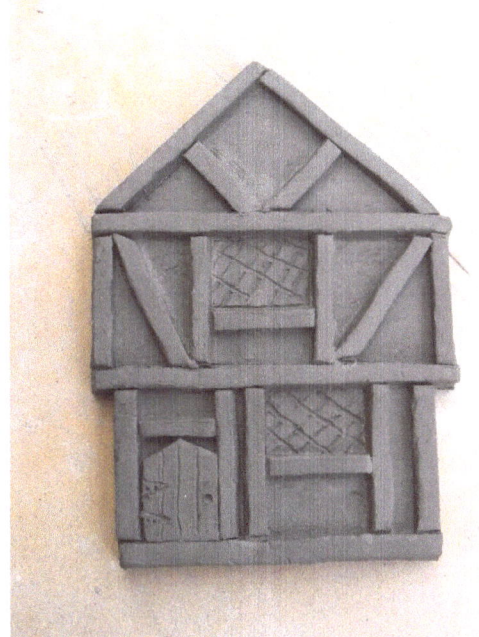

window sills, the lintel over the door and the diagonal supports.

Cut the ends either flat or at the correct angle depending on which piece you are fitting.

As we did earlier make and place the pieces in position then remove and stick each piece in turn remembering to make slip on both the house and the strip in each case.

**Decoration.**

There is very little decoration or embellishment left to do, just the door.

Use a sharp pencil to draw the door panels and the two door hinges, finally a small keyhole finishes it off.

Tudor House or Shop. Templates.

Note. Print this pdf page 'Actual Size@.

More projects from www.bmpotterycrafts.co.uk

Clay. House 330grams.

Strips from remaining clay. 3mm thick.

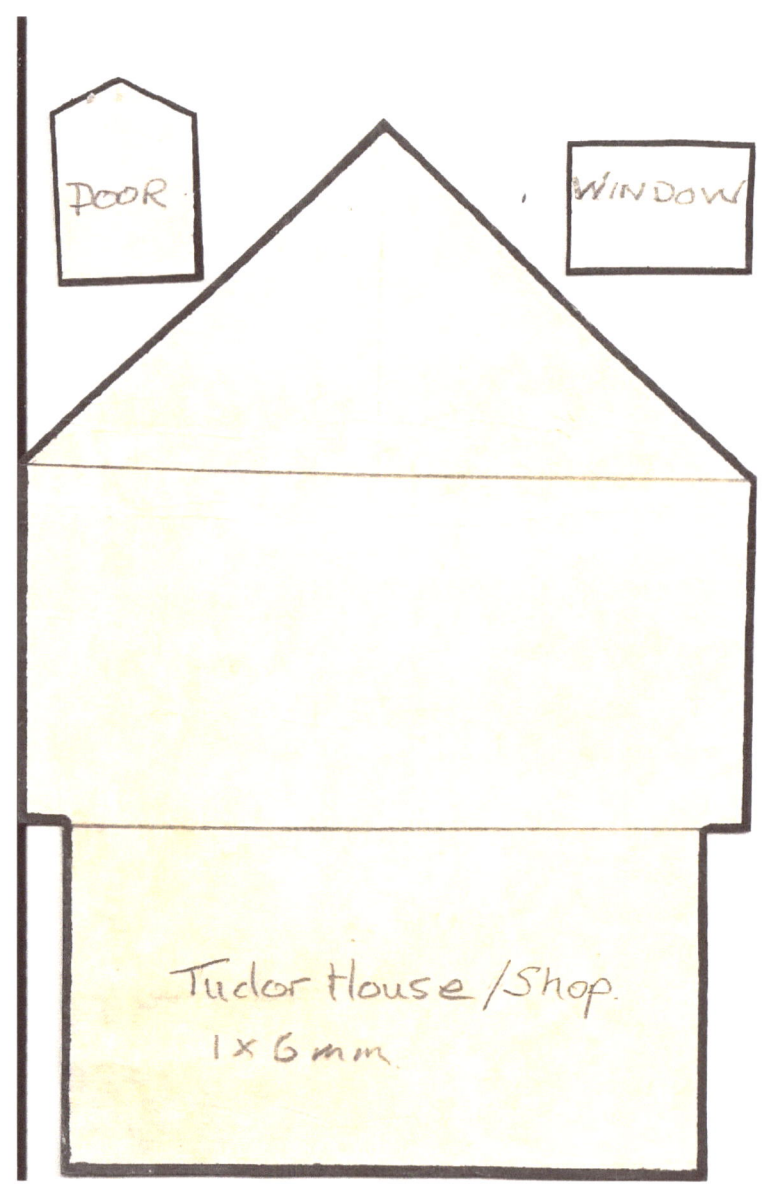

# Tudor Shop.

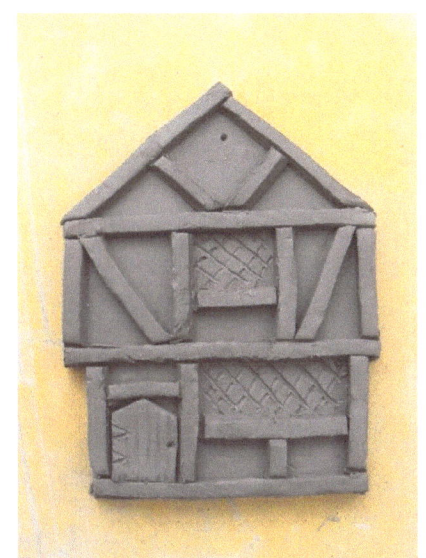

The construction of the **Tudor Shop** is exactly the same as the **Tudor House** until the section where we identify the windows.

The first floor window is the same but the ground floor shop window is stretched across the front of the building.

The elongated window is done using the same window template as before, this time touching the door post. Place the template alongside the doorpost and draw a line beneath it. Slide the template further across the window opening and continue the line right across the opening to position the window.

Continue cutting strips and complete the internal framework of the shop, remembering the support under the window frame.

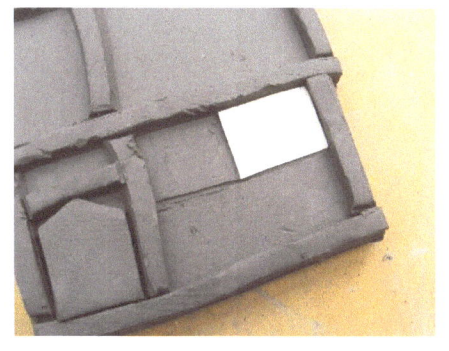

Decorate the window and door as we did with the house. Choose either a diamond or rectangular pattern for the windows.

**B & M Potterycrafts.**

The Tudor House demonstrating patterns is a larger version of the basic house and shop.

The larger structure allows pupils to incorporate a variation of patterns built into the structure.

Pupils can use vertical, horizontal or diagonal strips to enrich the model. It can be as simple or complex as they please within the constraints of the frame of the house, door and windows and depending on how narrow the strips can be produced.

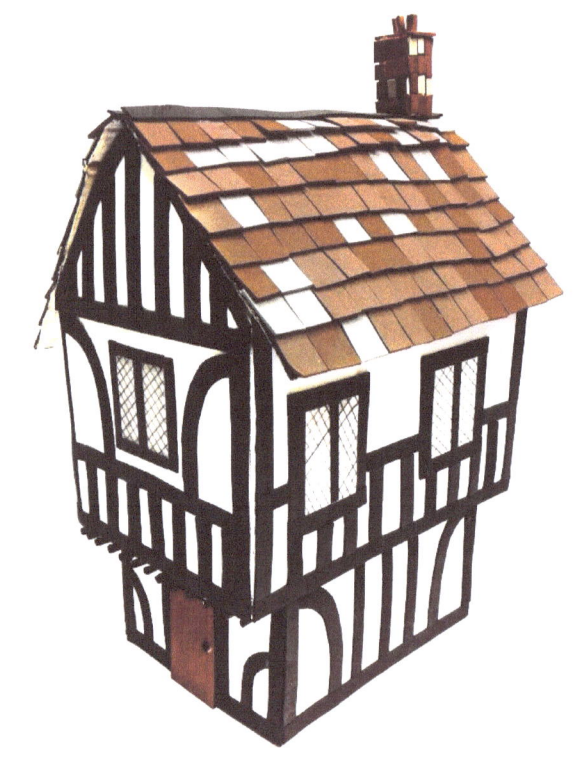

Sample of a more complicated Tudor house available from Google Images.

Demonstrating the range of patterns possible in your design.

Tudor House. Patterns. Clay 350 grams.

Note. Print this pdf page 'Actual Size'.

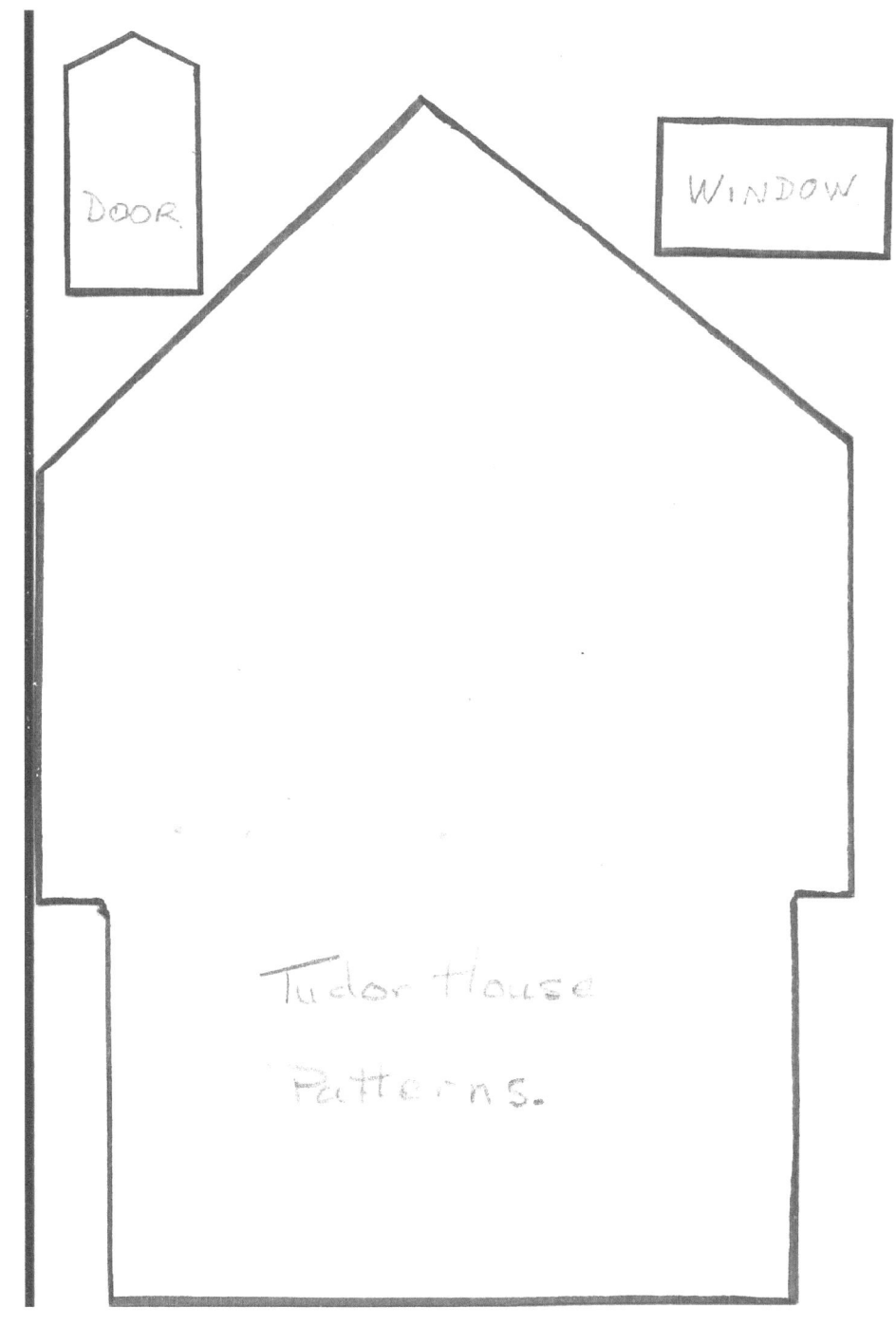

# B & M Potterycrafts.

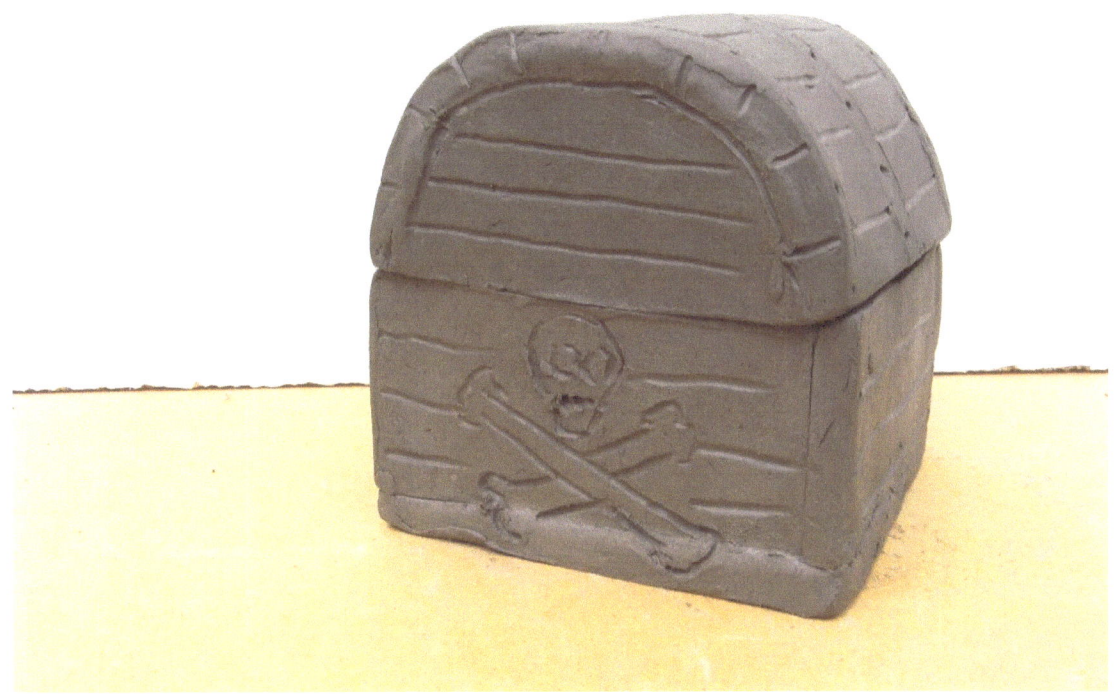

## Slab pot modelling projects.

## Pirate's treasure chest.

Create the model shown on this cover by following step by step, easy to understand instructions supported by still photos at each stage.

**Brian Rollins.**

More projects from :- www.bmpotterycrafts.co.uk

# B&M Potterycrafts.

# Building models in Clay.

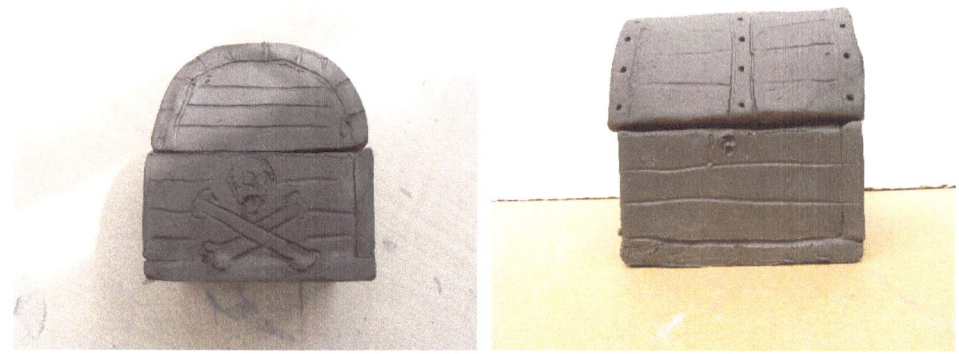

## Pirate Treasure Chest.

### Sequence

Generic skills.

Rolling the clay flat.

Cut out the pieces for the box.

Assemble the box.

Assemble the lid.

Decorate and design.

Complete the design.

**Roll out the clay and prepare the templates.**

**Page 4 to page 8.**

**Cut out the pieces for the box.**

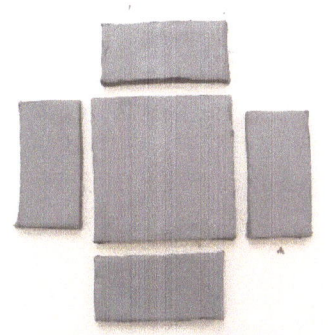

One square and four sides.

Place the templates on the clay and cut out the four rectangles and the square.

Templates should always be used with the plastic surface on the clay to stop the card soaking water from the clay and softening the surface.

As the surface is shiny it also helps to keep the template still by sticking where it touches while you are cutting around it.

To ensure that the template doesn't move during the cutting process hold it in place with one hand while cutting with the other hand.

Simply press the knife point through the clay and slide the blade along the work surface to ensure a clean cut, keeping the edge of the knife in contact with the template.

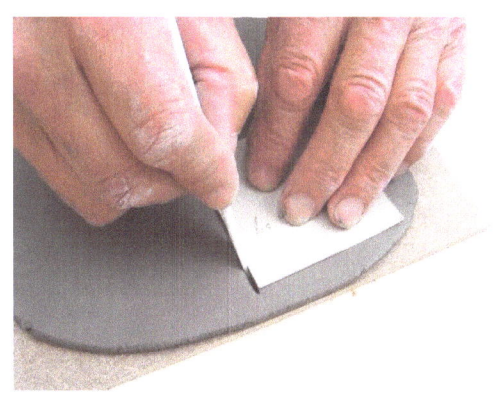

When making slab pot models it is important to keep the cutting edge vertical to the surface to be cut because if the knife is at an angle you will cut under one edge of the slab and over the other edge making it difficult to join cleanly to the next piece.

Try to cut in one clean motion, if you stop and restart you will probably leave a jagged edge.

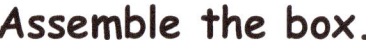

**Assemble the box.**

Lay out the pieces as shown in the picture,

Sides are slightly shorter than the base, allowing for the thickness of each side in the assembly.

Apply slip along one side of the base and on one edge of the side to be attached.

*The creation of **slip** is an important part of joining together two pieces of clay. The water from the brush is rubbed firmly into the clay surface until it turns a lighter grey colour this is the slip and acts as our glue.*

***Crosshatching** is one of the keys to joining two pieces of clay. It consists of the scoring the pieces in the areas to be joined. Use the point of the knife to score the clay.*

*The use of **pressure** is essential in successfully joining two pieces of clay when used in conjunction with crosshatching and slip.*

Press the side into position aligned with one edge of the base as shown. Slide the side slightly across the base with downward pressure to fix it firmly.

Always apply slip to both surfaces to be joined.

Apply slip along the next side of the base and on one edge of the side piece. This time add slip on the side already fixed to the base where it will touch the second side and on the corresponding edge of the second side piece. Press the side piece into the base and the two edges where they meet.

Make sure the sides align with the base.

Repeat his process with the other two sides remembering to apply slip to the edge of the first side before pressing the edge of the fourth side into place.

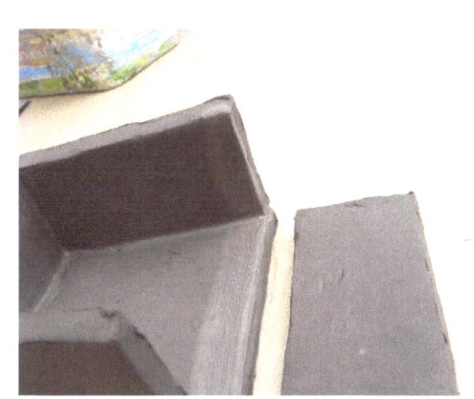

Smooth the joints along the edges of the box with your finger which makes a tidy finish and also strengthens the joints.

**Assemble the lid.**

Place the templates in position and cut out the pieces for the lid.

Two shapes are needed, one circle and one rectangle.

The rectangle is relatively simple to cut using the techniques outlined in the previous section.

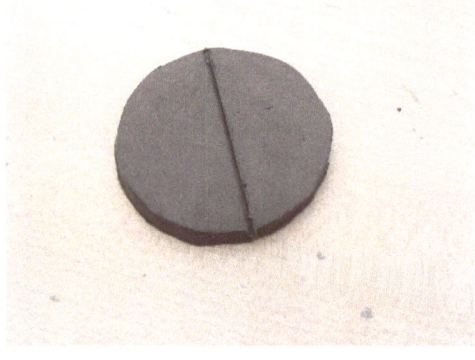

More care is needed with the circle, you will probably find it easier if you turn the work surface around as you use the knife, this will help you to keep the knife in an upright position while cutting the clay. After cutting out the circle shape draw a line across the middle of the circle and cut it in half when you are satisfied that the line is central.

Lay out the pieces as shown in the picture, the two longer edges house the semicircles which form the ends of the lid.

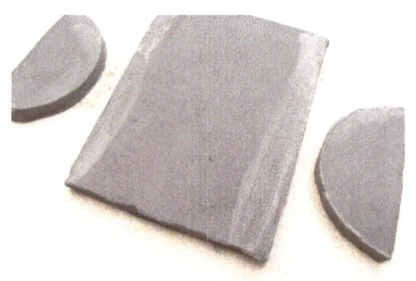

Create a 6mm line of slip along both of the long sides and around the rounded edges of the semi circles.

Place the centres of the semi circles lightly on the slip in

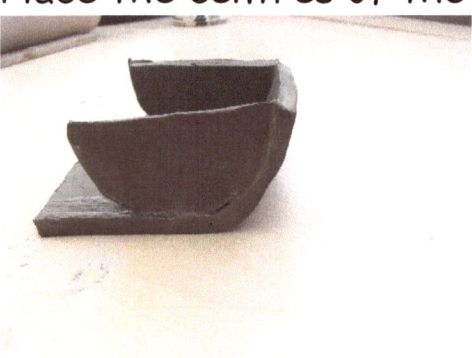

the middle of the edges and carefully fold the ends of the rectangle until they meet the semi circles.

The slip will hold the lid together while you check and adjust the positioning.

When you have lined up the pieces press the semi circles into place and smooth the joints with finger pressure.

While the clay is still relatively soft you can adjust the rounded shape of the lid and check that the lid sits flat on the chest.

**Decorate and design.**

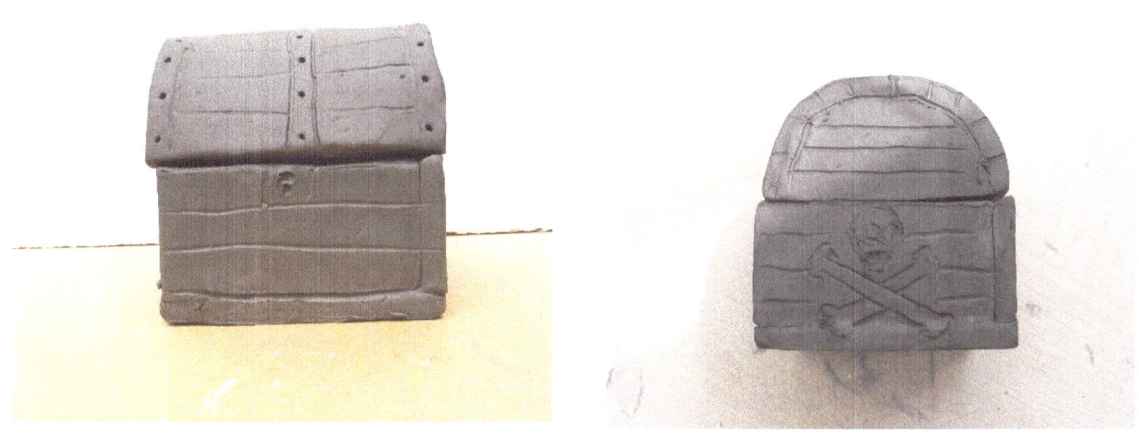

You can make the design on the treasure to look like the old pirate chest made from strong pieces of wood held together by iron bands riveted through the wood.

Patterns are made by carefully drawing the iron bands around the box and the lid with a sharp pencil or a small pointed stick.

Don't press too deeply into the clay just make the designs on the surface of the clay.

The rivets are simulated by making dots at regular intervals along the iron bands.

Finish off the design by drawing a key hole at the top of the box close by the lid.

You can also draw the pirate's skull and cross bone sign if you wish.

The same box shape with flower patterns on the lid also makes a fine jewellery box.

**Jewelery box suggestion.**

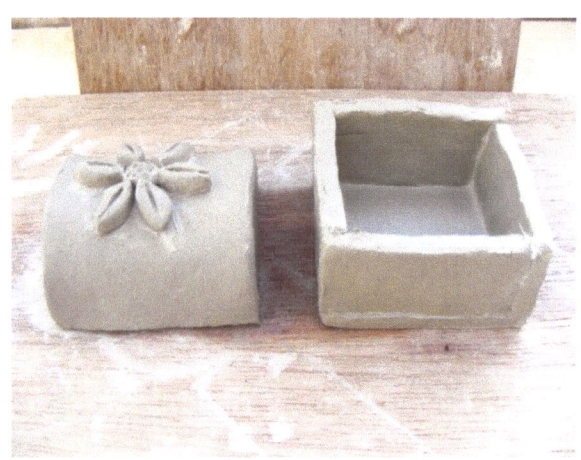

# B & M Potterycrafts.

Treasure Chest. Templates.

Clay 300gram.s 6mm thick.

Note. Print this pdf page 'Actual Size'.

Base x1. 6.5 cm square.

Sides x4. 5.7x3cm.

Lid x1. 6.5x9cm.

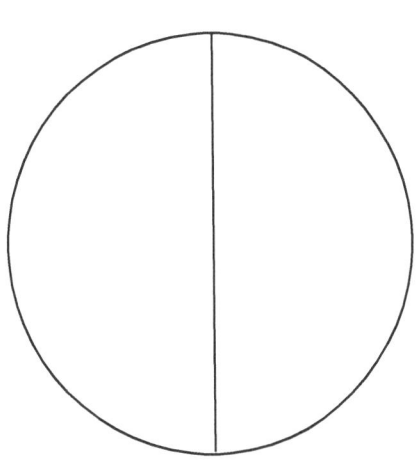

Lid sides x1. 5.5cm dia.

# B & M Potterycrafts.

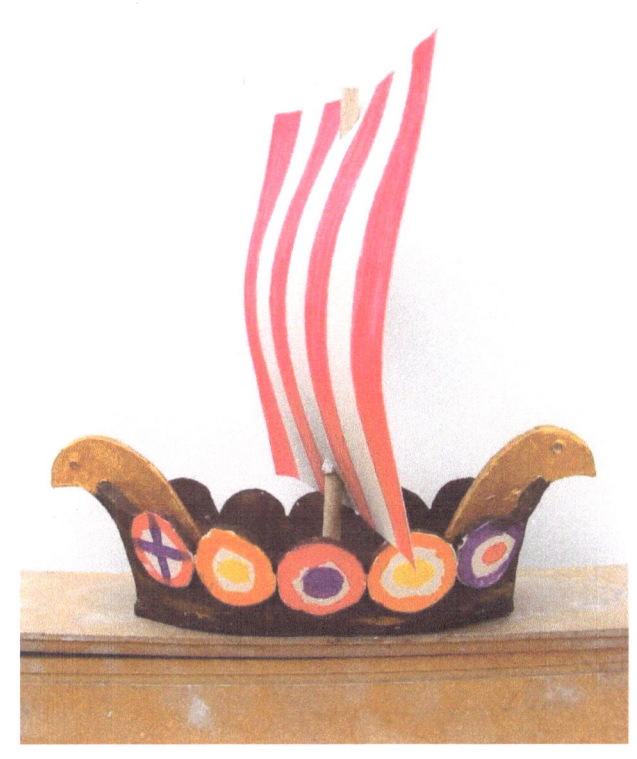

## Slab pot modelling projects.

## Viking boat.

Create the model shown on this cover by following step by step, easy to understand instructions supported by still photos at each stage.

**Brian Rollins.**

More projects from :- www.bmpotterycrafts.co.uk

# B&M Potterycrafts.

# Slab pot modelling projects.

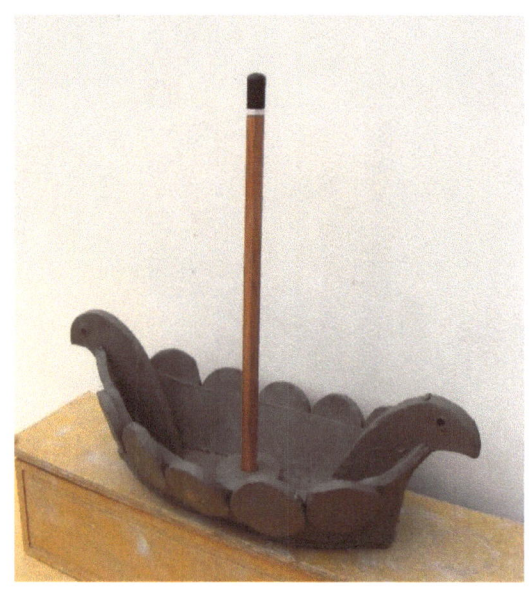

## Viking boat.

Sequence and contents.

Rolling the clay flat.

Preparation of templates.

Cut out the pieces.

Assemble the boat.

Make and fit the shields.

Decorate and design.

Worksheets.

Materials, Work Surfaces and Tools.

B & M Potterycrafts 2016.

**Roll out the clay and prepare the templates.**

**Page 4 to page 8.**


**Cut out the pieces.**

We are making a Viking boat which consists of an ovoid shaped base with two long curved pieces representing the sides of the boat and two smaller curved pieces to make the dragons head prows and stern of the boat.

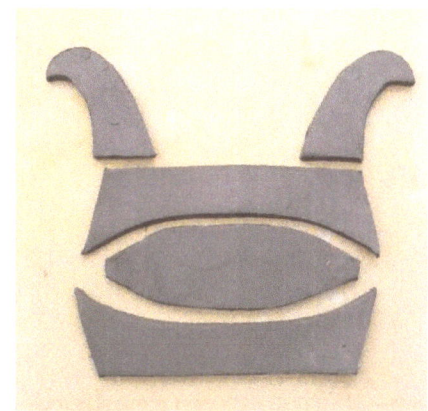

As you can see from the picture the model is made up from five separate shapes.

The ovoid shape for the bottom of the boat. Along each rounded side of the base we attach the flat edge of the sides. The flat edges of the dragon's head are fixed to the base and the boat is sealed by fixing the sides to the dragon's head. Shields are fixed along each side of the boat and two rings are stuck together and attached to the middle of the boat to stand the mast upright.

Place the templates on the clay and cut out the large pieces first.

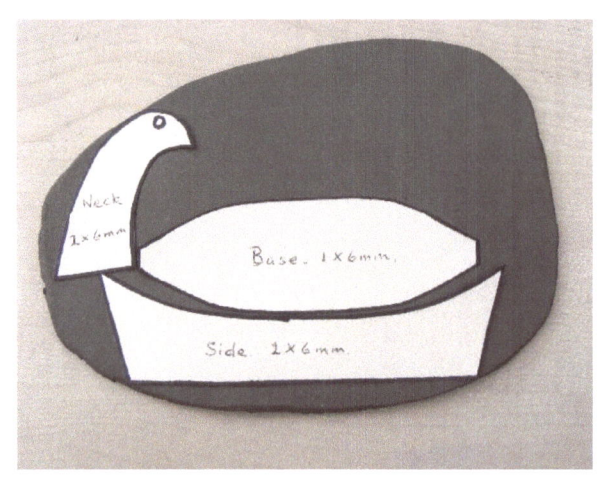

I always use the strategy of cutting large parts first, selecting pieces in reducing sizes. The reasoning behind this is that if you cut out the larger pieces first the slabs of clay remaining will be big enough to cut out all or some of the smaller pieces.

However this is less likely to be true if you leave the large piece to the last.

Templates should always be used with the plastic surface on the clay surface to stop the card soaking up water from the clay and softening the card.

As the surface is shiny it also helps to keep the template in place by sticking where it touches while you are cutting around it.

To ensure that the template doesn't move during the cutting process hold it in place with one hand while cutting with the other hand.

It is not vital that all the pieces are cut from that sheet in one go, if you cannot make a piece or pieces from the bits of clay left simply roll the bits into a smooth ball, pat it flat and roll it out again to cut out the last pieces.

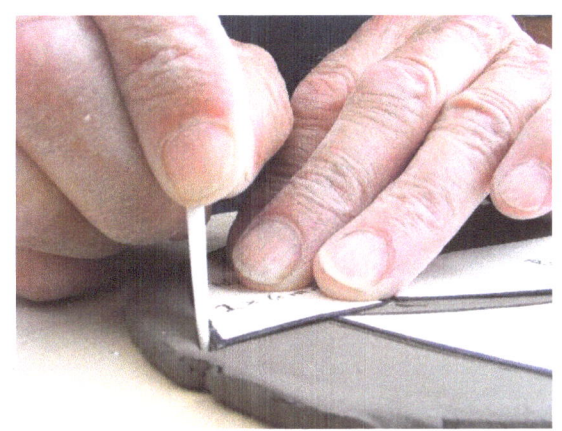

Hold the knife as if you were using a pencil that is with your fingers as close to the point as possible. This gives you more control of the knife point and stops the flexible plastic knife bending away from the clay.

Simply press the knife point through the clay and slide the blade along the work surface to ensure a clean cut, keeping the edge of the knife in contact with the template.

When making slab pot models it is important to keep the cutting edge vertical to the surface to be cut because if the knife is at an angle you will cut under one edge of the slab and over the other edge making them thin in places and difficult to join cleanly to the next piece.

Try to cut in one clean motion, if you stop and restart you will probably leave a jagged edge.

**Assemble the boat.**

Crosshatch, slip and pressure.

Three important parts to building clay models.

## *Crosshatching.*

The crosshatching serves to break up the surface of the model allowing water and therefore slip to penetrate deeper into the surface.

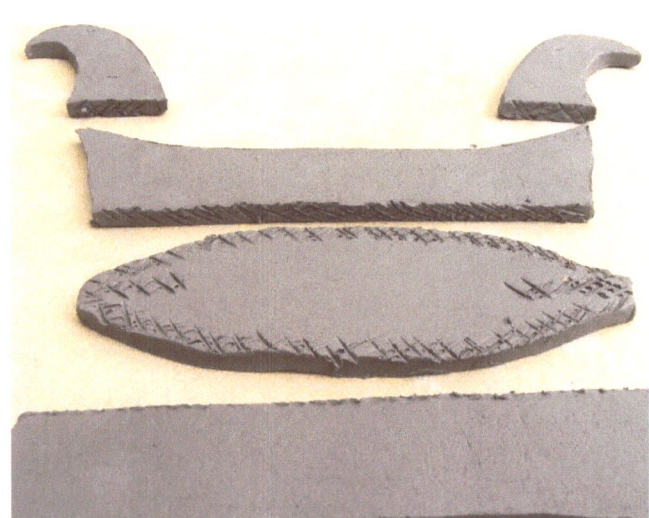

Hold the tip of your knife in your fingers as you would hold a pencil and score the surface of the clay with the sharp edge and point, this grip is demonstrated in the picture above which showed you how to cut the clay.

As you can see in the picture the crosshatch marks are made on each area that is going to be joined to another area and score marks are made in two directions giving the crosshatched pattern shown.

Along the top edges of the base where the boat sides are going to fit and at each end in the base where the dragon's necks are fitted.

When using crosshatching to join pieces of clay together it is best practice to crosshatch both surfaces.

Applying this rule you will see that the long straight edges of the boat sides are crosshatched as are the straight edges of the dragon's necks.

Crosshatching the base is quite straightforward, place the base on the work surface and holding the knife as described carefully score the clay in two directions.

Crosshatching the long edges of the boat sides and the dragon's necks is more complicated, you need to hold the strip of clay in one hand and hold the knife in the other hand while you score in one 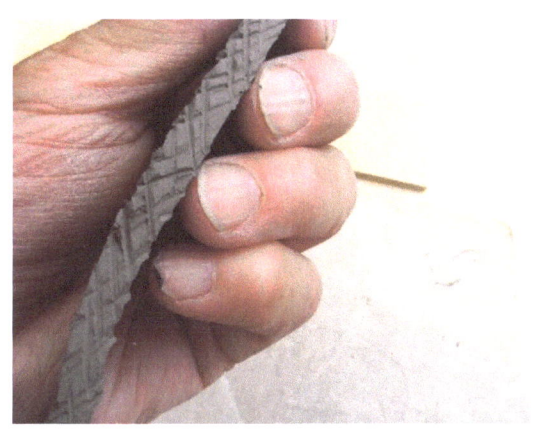 direction then turn the clay around to score across the first marks.

### Create slip.

Slip is the medium that helps the pieces bond together and 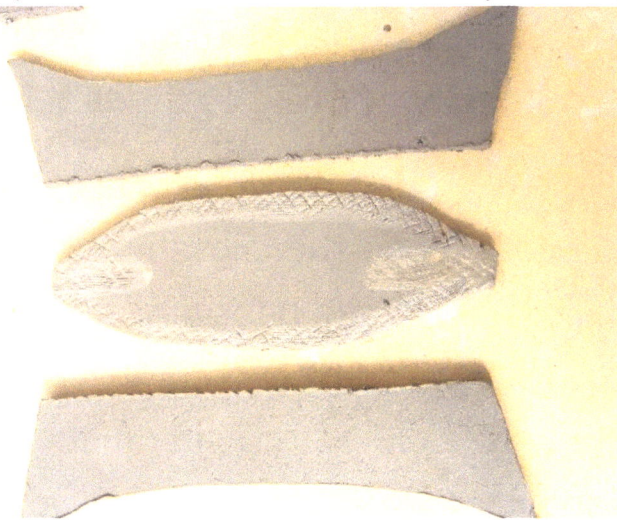 in making this model we will make the slip in situ that is in the spot where we need it for binding the pieces together.

To make the slip we use stiff nylon brushes and water.

Dip the brush in the water container and transfer the water onto the clay where you are making the slip. Firmly brush the water across and into the crosshatch marks until the surface changes to a lighter grey colour.

Keep the surfaces sticky until you join them together.

Start the assembly process with the two neck pieces.

Create slip in the two areas at the front and back of the boat and on the flat ends of the necks.

While the slip is still sticky press the first piece into the slip at one end of the boat applying **pressure** between the neck and the base by holding the piece between fingers and thumb as demonstrated in the picture, a slight rocking motion at the same time as the pressure helps the clay to remould and form a solid clay joint.

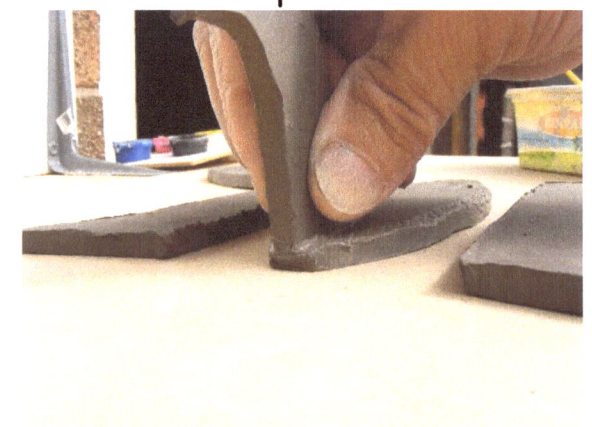

Repeat this process with the second neck, fixing these

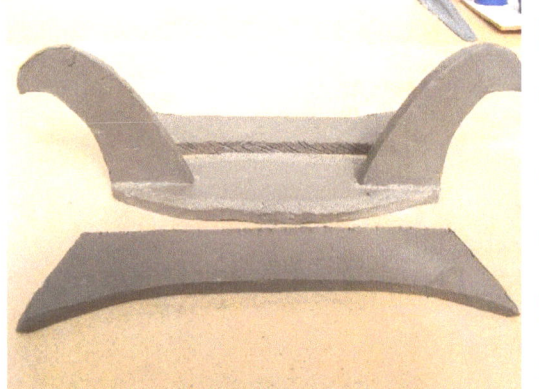

pieces provides support for the assembly of the two sides.

Create slip with your brush and water along the crosshatched portion of the base where the sides are to be fitted. Apply slip to one side of the base and by holding the side piece in the same manner as when you crosshatched it create slip along the edge.

Again using fingers at one side of the piece and thumb on the other side press the boat side firmly into position. Make sure that the side pieces are aligned with the two ends of the boat and that the sides follow the curved line of the base.

Do not fix the front and back edges to the neck until you are sure that both side are in the correct places.

Repeat this process with the second side, again check that it is fixed firmly to the base and that it follows the same curved line of the base.

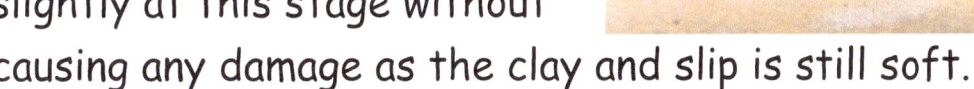

You can adjust the positioning slightly at this stage without causing any damage as the clay and slip is still soft.

The next part of the assembly is to attach the ends of the boat sides to the neck.

If you refer to the picture you will see that because the

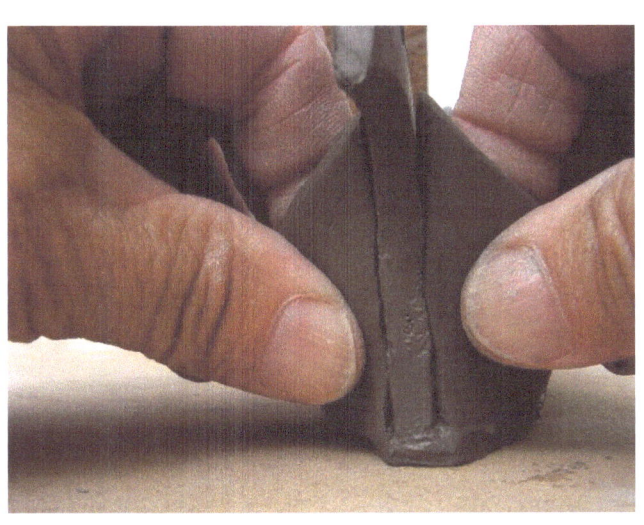

clay is still soft and wet you can carefully turn and bend it until the cut edges of the sides are touching the front of the neck piece.

Adjust the clay carefully a bit at a time until you achieve this position.

Complete the assembly of this first end by opening the space between the sides and the neck and creating slip on the front edges of the neck and on the flat edge of the side piece. When you have created sufficient slip hold the sides between fingers and thumbs as demonstrated and press the side piece into the slip on the neck. Doing both sides at the same time means that you can apply pressure from the sides into the neck to form a firm joint.

With finger pressure blend the clay from the sides into the neck which seals and strengthens the joint. Crosshatching is not used as modelling the joint in the manner shown makes a good strong joint.

Repeat this process with the assembly of the other end of the boat following the same steps.

This now means that you have a complete boat shape sealed at both ends all we need to do now is to strengthen the joints and further adjust the shape.

Strengthening the joints is done by applying finger pressure to the joints by sliding the tip of a finger along each joint and sealing it with pressure. This can be done inside and outside the boat if you can get your fingers in to the joint.

The method of assembly used means that the sides of our boat is a upright and as Viking boats are shaped very much like large canoes we need to lower the sides and widen the

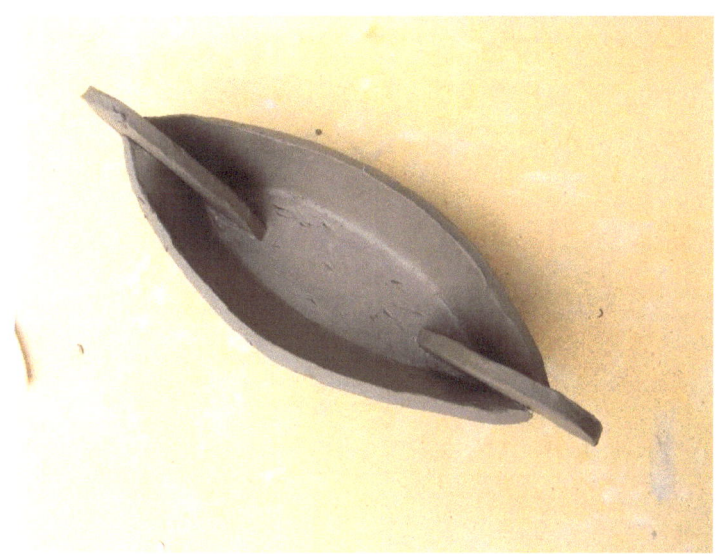

open top of the boat to look like the picture.

Carefully press the sides outward holding the sides with your fingers and thumbs forming and supporting both sides as you press outwards.

You can see from the picture that I have smoothed and strengthened the joints along the sides with finger pressure.

**Make and fit the shields.**

The shields are depicted by simple circles of clay and are fitted along both sides of the boat, for storage while at sea and for defence if the Vikings were under attack from arrows or spears.

We are fitting five shields along each side of the boat, starting with one in the centre and adding two font and two more back on both sides.

As I said the shields are simple circles cut from another, thinner, slab of clay.

Make the slab of clay using the techniques described earlier in the book.

This piece of clay is 3mm thick in order to make the shields lighter.

Roll out the slab and cut out ten shields plus two extra disks which we will stick together in the centre of the base to hold the mast. As soon as you have cut out the disks and while the clay is still moist you can position the shields along the sides before you stick them in place.

Start with the first shield in the centre with half of the shield above the side of the boat, as shown in the picture.

We are not using slip at this point merely finding the correct positions. With the clay still moist the shields will hold onto the side while you adjust the positions.

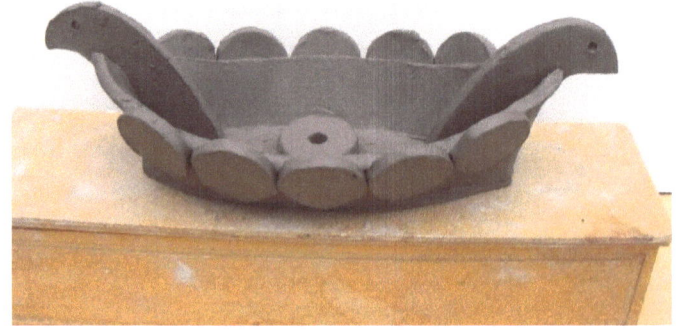

When you are satisfied that the first shield is central and at the correct height place the rest of the shields in position adding them one by one towards he front and back of the boat.

Having placed them as shown in the picture remove them one by one, make slip on half the shield add slip to the side of the boat in the empty spot and replace the shield and fix it back into place by gently squeezing it onto the boat's side with your finger and thumb.

Repeat this sticking process, one by one until all the shields are fixed and checked for position.

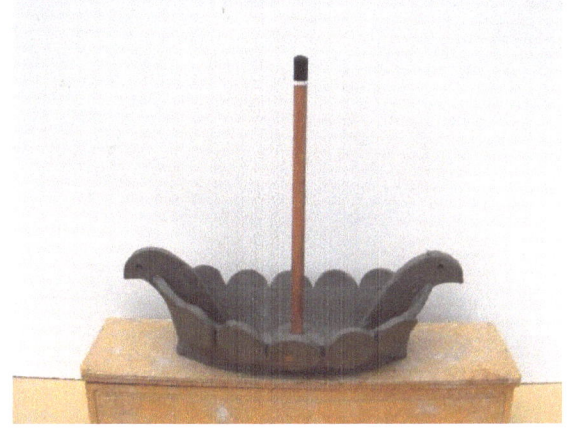

Create slip in the centre of the base and slip on one side of one disc and press it into position with pressure from your thumb. Make slip on top of that disc and on one side of the second disk and press the second one on top of the first one. This makes the boss which holds the mast.

While the clay is still soft push the mast into the clay to make a hole through the boss and into the base which will make it deep enough to hold the mast upright.

Please note that the clay will shrink as it is drying and also if the model is fired so the 6mm mast or pencil will need to be tapered, similar to sharpening the pencil a little, to hold the mast in the hole.

**Decoration.**

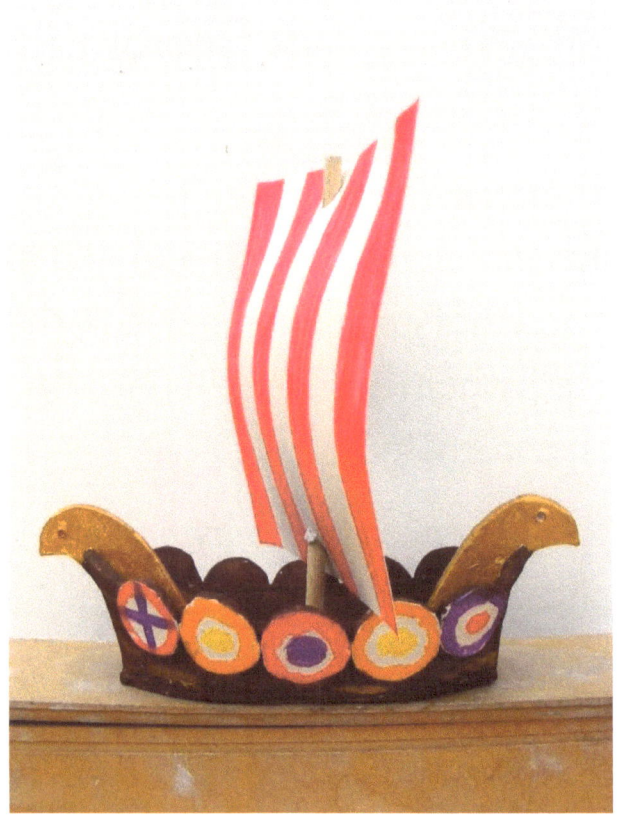

Most of the Viking boat's decoration is on the sail and on the shields.

The boat itself can be painted to simulate wood while the sails were usually made with vertical striped cloth, generally red and white.

Shields were decorated with personalised designs with strong colours consisting mainly of concentric circles.

# B & M Potterycrafts.

Viking Long Ship. Templates

Note. Print this .pdf page 'Actual Size

More projects from www.bmpotterycrafts.co.uk

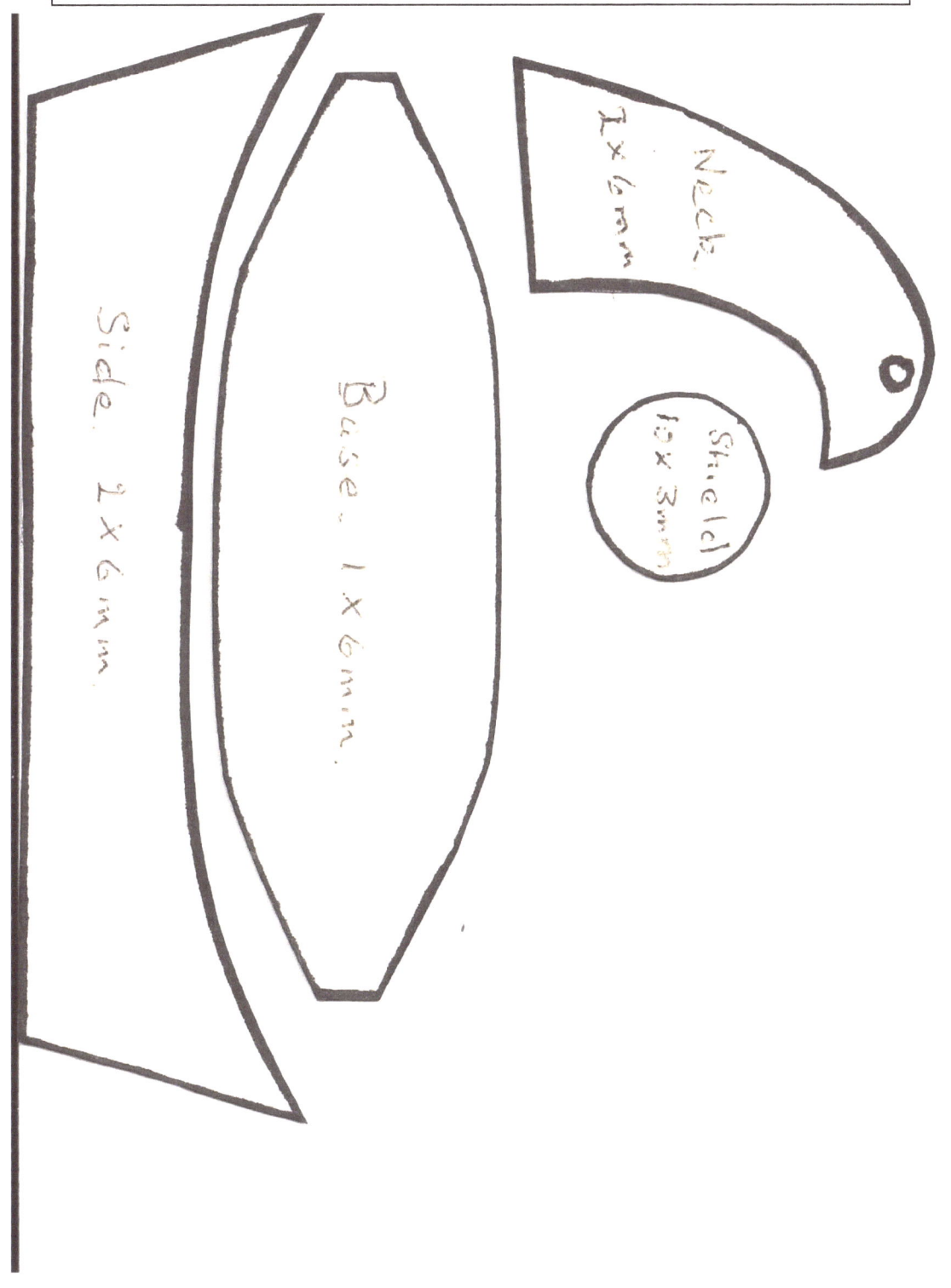

Side. 1 x 6 mm

Base. 1 x 6 mm.

Neck. 1 x 6 mm

Shield 10 x 3 mm

www.ingramcontent.com/pod-product-compliance
Lightning Source LLC
Chambersburg PA
CBHW050757180526
45159CB00003B/1491